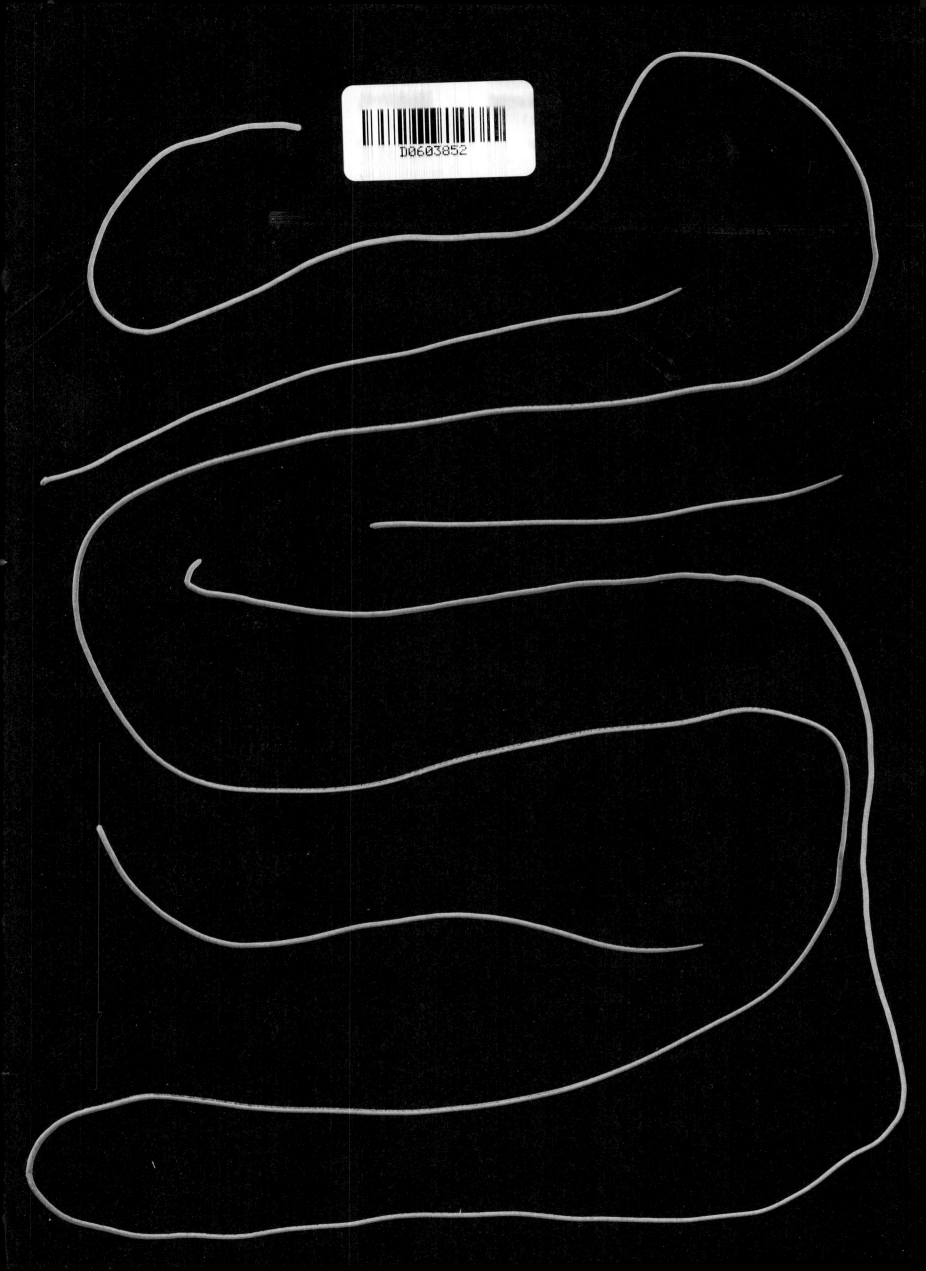

KENTUCKY II

KENTUCKY II

PHOTOGRAPHY BY JAMES ARCHAMBEAULT

TEXT BY THOMAS D. CLARK

To Owen & Leslie,
Hope you enjoy this vision
of Kentucky.
Merry Christmas, 1990
James Archambeault

GRAPHIC ARTS CENTER PUBLISHING COMPANY, PORTLAND, OREGON

International Standard Book Number 1-55868-013-6
Library of Congress Catalog Number 89-85592
© MCMLXXXIX by Graphic Arts Center Publishing Company
P.O. Box 10306 • Portland, Oregon 97210 • 503/226-2402
Editor-in-Chief • Douglas A. Pfeiffer
Associate Editor • Jean Andrews
Designer • Robert Reynolds
Cartographer • Tom Patterson and Manoa Mapworks
Typographer • Harrison Typesetting, Inc.
Printer • Dynagraphics, Inc.
Bindery • Lincoln & Allen
Printed in the United States of America

Dedicated to the memory of Secretariat,
whose spirit embodies all that is Kentucky.

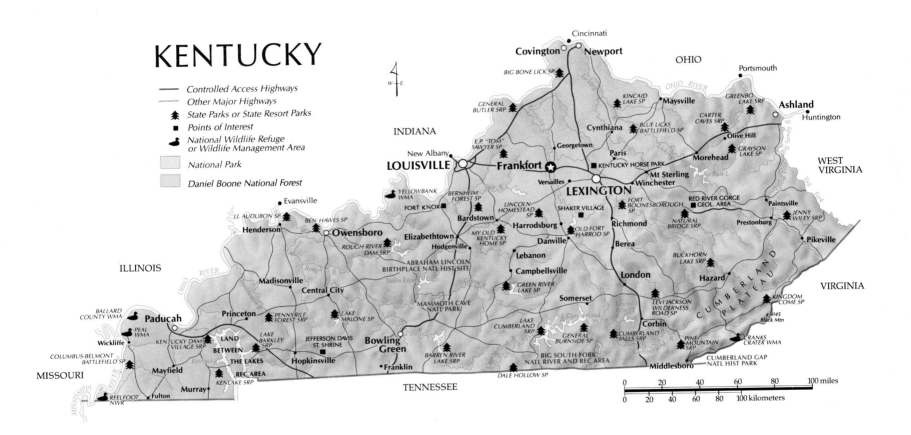

■ *Frontispiece:* On the first Saturday in May, the world watches the Kentucky Derby at Churchill Downs in Louisville. This most famous of horse races first saw three-year-old thoroughbreds flying around the track in 1875. ■ *Right:* Redbud and dogwood briefly mingle their blooms in central Kentucky's Madison County.

■ *Left:* Father and son enjoy an afternoon of fishing in one of Kentucky's hundreds of fine fishing streams. ■ *Above:* Whitetail deer leave their daytime cover to graze. With better game management and an aggressive stocking program, the state's deer population is increasing. ■ *Overleaf:* Western Kentucky's hill country is a mixture of woodlots flanked by pastures. Here, common fescue grows in Daviess County.

■ Kentucky has many pilot knobs, high points where Indians and early pioneers looked across great distances. This view, on a humid summer morning near Pilot Knob in Berea, Madison County, shows the small farms that dot the western foothills of the Appalachian Mountains. Farms like these preserve many Appalachian traditions.

■ *Above:* Sunrise gilds Barren River Lake State Resort Park in Allen County, in the state's southcentral region. Kentucky's fifteen resort parks and twenty state parks attract millions of visitors. ■ *Overleaf:* Mares and foals graze lazily in a pasture of bluegrass on the border of Fayette and Scott counties. Kentucky is a leader in raising thoroughbreds, breeding thousands annually in a cycle that dates back two hundred years.

■ The Kentucky River cuts a deep path through the limestone of central Kentucky. The river's Palisades region resembles the Kentucky pioneers saw. It is a land of steep cliffs, thick forests, many small tributaries, and a variety of plants, wildflowers, and wild game. Pioneers called it Eden. Indians called it the Land of Tomorrow.

■ Late September ushers in the first hint of autumn along the South Elkhorn Creek. This creek eventually joins North Elkhorn Creek to form the beautiful Elkhorn Creek, a pristine tributary of the Kentucky River. Early settlers established claims along this and other shallow, limestone runs, building fine farms and the prospering county towns of Paris, Georgetown, Nicholasville, Richmond, Winchester, and Versailles.

■ White fences and flowering trees lead to the grand barn of the Manchester Farm near the Keeneland Race Course in Lexington. Central Kentucky's Bluegrass region numbers hundreds of horse farms, many of them graced with Georgian and Greek Revival homes. Lush pastures support some of the world's finest thoroughbreds, standardbreds, quarter horses, saddle horses, and Arabians.

KENTUCKY

Kentucky is pitching headlong into its third century as an organized commonwealth and into a new era in its history. From this pinnacle of time, its people stand as though on the peak of Black Mountain, looking back into the past and peering anxiously into the future.

Kentuckians stoutly cherish the memories of their forebears who conquered the wilderness and established homes and farms. They glory in their pioneer legends and folklore and in the many heroic images created over the years. *Frontier* has ever been a starred word in their lexicon. Fortunately, this generation of Kentuckians is best equipped of any to take a look into its history. Assembled in voluminous files of yellowing records in the Kentucky State Archives and in the University of Kentucky's Special Collections are the documentary sources which describe a people creating their own unique regional way of life. Buried in the long ranges of leather-bound books and in voluminous cases of loose records is the official story of a people at all stages of history.

Here they are, carving corn fields out of the woods, erecting pole cabins, double-log houses, and Greek Revival mansions; building on a maze of Indian and buffalo trails a network of modern highways; raising electric generating plants and high dams; vastly expanding the state's water surface in elongated, impounded lakes; and creating cities, towns, and villages that today hold slightly more than half of Kentucky's population.

Geographically, Kentucky has been as much a keystone state as Pennsylvania. A peculiar "humped camel" conformation nestled between the western rivers and the pine-capped eastern Appalachian highlands, it dips as far south as the low-lying lands of the Mississippi Basin. Historically, Kentucky has been neither Southern nor Northern in tradition or politics. Like a wayward daughter, it has taken a willful and independent road, sometimes to its own disadvantage.

Because its elongated shape cuts across several distinct geological and geographical lines, Kentucky has never been drawn into a tightly knit social and political whole. Although historians, political scientists, sociologists, and creative writers have responded to this fact, thus far, no writer has been able to compress the profile of the state between the covers of a single book. Novelists have written capably and extensively of region and section, but none has written *the* Kentucky novel.

There has, however, been a particular quality, real or imagined, of land, nature, and human characters that has appealed to Kentucky writers. Kentucky's relatively dismal standing in economic and educational statistical tables reveals little about the state's real qualities; and this fact has stimulated the writing and publishing of local books.

Just as early pioneers struggled against the odds to settle Kentucky in the closing of the eighteenth century, their descendants are now caught up in crusades of self-improvement to enter the twenty-first with comparable courage. Kentuckians are not unaware of changes which are going on in the world about them; they seek the best means to accept new things without losing old, cherished values. Once a predominately rural region, nurturing an agrarian turn of mind, Kentucky now sees current statistics tilting against traditional ways of life. Today, more Kentuckians are classed urban or nonfarm-rural than are classed rural. Such revolutionary changes take a heavy toll of the Kentucky sense of values, and of the memories of other days.

Five interstate highways penetrate Kentucky from several directions and daily carry traffic into and through the state. Even a temporary blockage of Interstate 75 can halt enough human and commercial traffic to populate and stock with goods a middle-sized county. Kentucky has had some success in holding at arm's length billboard advertisers, so modern travelers following the highway, a route parallel to Daniel Boone's famous 1775 trail from Cumberland Gap to Fortress Boonesboro, can sense the lay of the land over which the pioneers straggled into the western country. A visitor might even share famous Bluegrass author James Lane Allen's sensations of 1885. This early American author of the local colorist school journeyed on horseback from Lexington to Cumberland Gap via Burnside and Cumberland Falls. Allen was a Bluegrass provincial who had been to New York but never out to the other sections of Kentucky. On the Cumberland River, standing before the "craggy face" of Anvil Rock, he was lulled into a trance by the beauty of his surroundings. Later he wrote:

> The utter silence and heart oppressing repose of primeval nature around us. The stark white and gray trunks of the immemorial forest dead linked us to an inviolable past. The air seemed to blow upon us from regions illimitable and unexplored, and to be fraught with unutterable suggestions. The full moon swung itself aloft over the sharp touchings of the green with spectral pallor; and the evening-star stood lustrous on the western horizon in depths of blue as cold as a sky of Landseer, except where brushed by the tremendous shadows of rose on the verge of the sunlit world.

A century before James Lane Allen reached realization, others had stood on the pinnacle of Cumberland Gap and other Kentucky mountain peaks, had walked across limestone and sandstone cliffs and round rock-strewn stream banks, and had been transfixed by the scene which rolled out before them. They traveled along the Kentucky, Big Sandy, Licking, Green, Barren, Cumberland, and Tennessee rivers, beholding landscapes as varied as the social and sectional organizations the Commonwealth would eventually build. French adventurers who early in the eighteenth century arrived on the banks of the Ohio were so entranced that in a burst of Gallic emotions they named it *la Belle Rivière,* and it has ever remained one of America's truly magnificent streams.

It was not by accident that the artist who designed the noble federal-style statehouse in Frankfort reserved the east and west lunettes for symbolic scenes of the Commonwealth's early history. One of these memorializes long hunters peering out over a broad, rolling countryside as viewed from atop the vantage point of a pilot knob. The other shows two settlers joining hands in a classic gesture of unity. In both, the artist embodied the spirit of virginal Kentucky, a land of wide vistas whether viewed from a steep ridge or from the vantage point of history.

For Kentucky, nature has been both generous and long-suffering. Surely, the primeval forest must have impressed even those Stone Age men who tramped over its floor, lived on its ridge tops and in rock houses, hunted and fished its streams, raised mounds over their dead, and chiseled millions of arrow and spear points and other tools from native stones. Along with the buffalo and deer, they padded out a veritable network of paths from Cumberland Gap north, across fords, and from one salt lick to another. They set seasonal fires to stimulate the growth of grass and cane and engaged in elementary agriculture. When the earliest Anglo-Americans crossed over into the western littoral, entering the wilderness through the gateways of the Ohio River and the Cumberland Gap, they entered a trail-dense country.

At some unrecorded time, and by a nameless person, the buffalo-warrior trace leading north was named the "Wilderness Road." This ancient highway burrowed its way through one of the noblest stands of hardwoods to be found on the North American continent, perhaps on the globe. The modern imagination is challenged to call up a vision of the sentinel trees of the forest, but one thing is certain: the primeval Kentucky forest setting was one for all seasons, and fitting for changing human moods. In dormant seasons, spreading gray branches of ancient trees capped the landscape with the melancholic pattern and shadings of nature's artistry. In burgeoning spring, the woods budded and bloomed in rich canopies of green promise.

In early spring, the Kentucky forest lives at two seasonal levels. In the earliest season, the understudy blooms, and flowering plants and shrubbery monopolize their moment in the sun. Well before it sends out fresh leaf buds, the "sarvice" berry has sprinkled the Kentucky

Canadian geese, Lake Barkley, Land Between the Lakes

woods with patches of white bloom, a certain omen that spring is on its way. From the ground spring up trillium of half a dozen hues, wild iris, jack-in-the-pulpit, May apple, snakeroot, and wild violets. Ferns and patches of rare ground-cedar keep the promise of life throughout the year, spreading a rich emerald carpet over rock outcroppings and acid-ladened humus beds. Then, in the time of leafing-out, the oaks, buckeyes, tulip poplars, ash, hickories, and maples spread a ceiling that shuts out the sun, and the understudy plants sink back into a long period of dormancy.

Between the New Madrid Bend of the Mississippi in the Jackson Purchase, and the depths of the Breaks of Sandy in the east, nature arranged the Kentucky fauna in a highly variegated tapestry. There are plants which thrive in the swamplands about Reelfoot Lake that would perish in a moment on the rock-bound highlands, and highland plants that cannot tolerate the environment of the bog. Across the Cumberland River to the east, the aromatic ground plant, pennyroyal (pennyrile to the natives), has given its name to a broad land, while in central Kentucky, the rich limestone plateau bears the name of its bright-green grass. The history of this "bluegrass" is shrouded in some

mystery. No one knows whether it is native or an import, but bluegrass has given its name to a region that is known wherever sporting horses are bred and raced.

No region of Kentucky produces so wide a variety of fauna as the Appalachian Highlands. Laurel and rhododendron create matted barriers, which in season become extravagant natural woods wreaths. The wahoo, or mountain magnolia, along with redbud, dogwood, flowering crab, wild plum, and sourwood, welcomes spring with bursts of brilliant color. Flowering with them is a plant that has about it an aura of romance and far-flung fame. Early in Kentucky's settlement ginseng became a precious treasure, as it was the only commodity that could be transported to an eastern market and yield a profit. For more than two centuries, lonely wanderers have moved through the damp mountain swales like gold and silver prospectors, digging the treasured, bulbous roots to be sold in China as an aphrodisiac.

Word of the rich fauna and flora in the Kentucky wilderness spread abroad at an early date. In time, a veritable army of naturalists, botanists, ornithologists, and others came searching for new scientific materials. No doubt many of their exaggerated descriptions, published abroad, stimulated immigration to North America. In 1791, Gilbert Imlay, the exuberant English traveler and immigrant agent, came down the Ohio to Kentucky. Later, he informed his English audience:

> Everything here assumes a dignity and splendor I have never seen in any other part of the world. You ascend a considerable distance from the Ohio, and when you suppose you have arrived at the summit of the mountain, you find yourself upon an extensive level. Here an eternal verdure reigns, and the brilliant sun of latitude 30°, piercing through the azure heavens, produces in prolific soil, an early maturity which is truly astonishing. Flowers full and perfect as if they had been cultivated by the hand of the florist.

Imlay may have been overzealous in describing Kentucky to his English readers. Perhaps the "soft zephyrs" he described blowing upon him had an intoxicating effect.

But the land Imlay saw was open promise for British and European botanists, who descended upon Kentucky in search of unclassified plants. Both André and François A. Michaux tramped the countryside, gathering specimens and attaching their names to them. Never before had these scientists seen such an extensive variety of plants and trees. François spent a good bit of time measuring sycamore trees and wrote that, "Kentucky is the native country of the tulip tree; between Beardstown (Bardstown), and Louisiana (Louisville) we saw a few spots in the woods, which consist of that tree alone."

The botanists, along with most other European visitors, traveled into Kentucky over the route of the "grand tour," which led from Maysville to Lexington, and then to Louisville. Scores of foreign and domestic travelers came this way, notebooks in hand, recording their experiences and the lay of the land. Some came to see how well settlers were reacting to the virgin western country; some, to see first-hand the operation of slavery; others, to advance trade and scientific missions. Nearly all of them complained about poor roads, poor inns, poor beds, and coarse-mannered people who bolted down their food and dashed away from the table almost before the landlord had quit ringing the dinner bell. The visitors included advance agents for immigration companies, scientists, General Lafayette (the Guest of the Republic), Alexis, Comte de Tocqueville (the famous political observer), General

López de Santa Anna (ostensibly a prisoner of war, who traveled as a guest of some notoriety, if no honor), and the famous English novelist, Charles Dickens. These, along with their lesser fellows, contributed an important body of contemporary observation on the new Kentucky.

Plodding along the Maysville-Lexington road before 1830, no traveler, local or foreign, could have imagined that the Maysville Road would become an interesting footnote in the history of American internal improvements. This route had been tramped out by Indians and buffalo centuries before, but by the midnineteenth century, the Maysville Road might have been labeled the route of the politicians. John Breckinridge, Henry Clay, and John Jordan Crittenden traveled it. Andrew Jackson and James Knox Polk rode it on their way to assume the office of the presidency. Earlier, General Lafayette traveled it from Lexington to Maysville. Henry Clay was so closely identified with it that the Maysville Road was said to be his private highway. In 1830, when Congress authorized the organization of a turnpike company, President Jackson vetoed the bill on the grounds that it served only one state, but in fact he opposed it because it served his nemesis, Henry Clay. This set back federal aid to American highways by a century.

Both the Wilderness and the Maysville roads cut across Kentucky's sectional lines to wind up in the Bluegrass. They poured visitors and settlers into a region which came to resemble parts of Virginia and even England. One particular resident gave the Bluegrass its architectural distinction. When Gideon Shryock returned from Philadelphia in 1825, he brought along in his intellectual baggage a new symbol befitting a prospering land. Shryock had gone away to study architecture under the famous Greek Revivalist, William Strickland. By a happy coincidence, Shryock arrived home when central Kentuckians were aroused over the Greek revolt against Turkish oppressors. Their interest had been nurtured by Transylvania University's curriculum, which was heavily weighted toward the study of the classics and by the nineteenth century's educational emphasis on Latin and ancient Greek.

Shryock's return home was propitious for another reason as well. Both the Kentucky statehouse and temporary legislative halls had been recently destroyed by fire. Arriving armed with the classics, the young architect was commissioned to design and build a new capitol—fireproof, and constructed of native stone—that would befit the dignity and aspirations of the Commonwealth. No sluggard, Shryock raised a classic Greek temple that could easily have graced any acropolis in the ancient world. This building duplicates the lines of the Parthenon in a New World setting.

Impressed by the new seat of Kentucky statehood, Transylvania University employed Shryock to design a structure evoking their classical curriculum. The result was a graceful American Sunium with its facing portico supported by six Doric columns. Shryock's faithfully reproduced Parthenon in Frankfort and his Sunium in Lexington set the style throughout the Bluegrass. Soon Doric and Corinthian columns adorned traditional Georgian structures, and pillared mansions became a symbol of Bluegrass style and affluence.

In the Bluegrass, fields and meadows yielded rich harvests of grain, hemp, and tobacco. Farms produced whiskey, prize livestock, and cured meats. Droves of hogs, flocks of sheep, herds of cattle, and numerous horses and mules were driven along the Wilderness Road and through the Cumberland Gap to the markets along the Atlantic Coast, and the down-river trade returned rich cash rewards. There was no better way of expressing these rich returns than by erecting farm manor houses behind lines of white columns and by adorning their interiors with personal art. Matthew Harris Jouett, Samuel Price,

Joseph H. Bush, Oliver Frazer, and others perpetuated human mainprize in hundreds of family portraits. An ancestral portrait painted by Matthew Harris Jouett was then, as it is now, a gilt-edged certification of aristocratic status. Sharing space on Bluegrass living- and dining-room walls were Edward Troye's portraits of named stallions and purebred bulls. The arts of architecture and painting witnessed the happy wedding of a rising country gentry to a rich, productive land. Beyond this, buildings and paintings evoked connections with the ancients and suggested that a country life-style akin to that of the English and Scottish gentry could be planted in the Bluegrass.

The Bluegrass region is fitted like a geographic jewel inside a setting of hills to the east and the Ohio Valley to the west. Here, much of Kentucky's social, economic, and political history has been generated. From this region came the state's best-known judges, lawyers, physicians, and merchants. Here began Kentucky's famous newspaper tradition, with John Bradford's *Kentucky Gazette* proving a seminal training ground for editors from Lexington to the Pacific Coast. In other fields, the influence of Kentucky and the Bluegrass also spread far: the Sublette brothers, four grandsons of the old Wilderness Road Indian

Centre Family Dwelling, Shaker Village, Pleasant Hill

fighter William Whitley, carried on their family tradition of trading fur in the Rocky Mountains; William Becknell helped open the Santa Fe trade route to New Mexico; and Susan Magoffin of Harrodsburg recorded a picturesque journal of her adventures on that trail. The wandering instinct has always been a strong one in Kentuckians.

At home, the dream of the "garden" for many a Bluegrass farmer or merchant came true. More than an economy, farming became a comfortable way of life, one in which you could experiment with plant and animal breeding. Men like Lewis Sanders and Robert Wilmot Scott distinguished themselves in both areas. Later, wealthy farmer-businessmen like E. H. Taylor and Ben Ali Haggin became distinguished cattle and horse breeders. Even Henry Clay, on his famous Ashland Estate, developed almost as great a reputation as a farmer and breeder as he did as a statesman. Thousands of heads of horses, cattle, sheep, and hogs were imported from abroad, and Kentucky became a center for improving and exporting purebred animals, including Kentucky shorthorn cattle, a breed which still exists. The aristocrats of farming and breeding gathered themselves into agricultural societies and racing associations and became promoters of scientific farming.

An outgrowth of their interest was the agricultural college and its associated animal and plant research bodies. Naturally, one of the agricultural bodies focused on raising and marketing burley tobacco.

Despite changes which have occurred in plant types, methods of disease control, control of acreage, and the marketing process, there survive vestiges of the old ways. When the burley is ready in the warehouses, auctioneers still march up and down long rows of baled tobacco chanting their unintelligible cries and they are still followed by great trails of farmers.

No greater contrast has existed in Kentucky than that between wealthy farmers in the Bluegrass and Pennyrile regions and small subsistence farms in other parts of the state. Though Kentucky has never been considered a plantation state, owners of fertile Bluegrass and Pennyrile farms have historically been masters of their world. Like the Bluegrass, the Pennyrile projects a pronounced regional personality and embodies the very essence of the state's rural-agrarian tradition. Its people have lived close to the land, yielding to its vagaries and turnings with warm affection. This rural heartland rolls out in a southwestward slant from Appalachia to the Cumberland River.

Standardbred mares, Almahurst horse farm, Jessamine County

The Pennyrile claims for its own some of Kentucky's most distinctive natural and human landmarks. The mysterious Barrens caught the attention first of the long hunters, and then of geologists, botanists, and historians. The caverns of the central area contain rich deposits left by Paleolithic people, sparkling cathedral-sized chambers, and an underground river of international fame. Visitors flock to National Mammoth Cave Park to explore the subterranean passages and caverns and to wander through the surrounding woodlands. In 1925, Floyd Collins, an ill-fated spelunker, became entrapped in a cavern passage and for the month before he died was the center of international news coverage.

Running like brilliant emeralds through the Pennyrile are the Barren and Green rivers. They are said to be the narrowest and deepest navigable streams on the continent. Upriver, Green County is a veritable museum collection of early Kentucky architecture, ranging from the simple pole cabin to the more sophisticated Georgian house.

The Pennyrile has given rise to a number of distinguished medical pioneers, statesmen, authors, and Kentucky-style politicians. It was from this region that Jane Todd Crawford rode horseback from Greensburg to Danville in 1809 to seek Dr. Ephriam McDowell's help.

When the doctor removed her twenty-pound tumor, he made medical history. In Hodgensville, on the western slope of the knobs, Abraham Lincoln was born, and Jefferson Davis came into the world in the fertile farming country on the Todd-Christian county border. Simon Bolivar Buckner, a famous Confederate General, and one of Kentucky's better governors, came from Munfordsville, and Arthur Krock, nationally respected political analyst, was a native of Barren County.

Three Pennyrile authors, Robert Penn Warren of Guthrie, Janice Holt Giles of Knifely, and Eliza Calvert (Hall) Obenchain of Bowling Green, have written vividly of the region. In *Night Rider, World Enough and Time*, and a reminiscent volume about his father, Warren "returned home" and evoked a profound sense of longing. In *The Enduring Hills*, Janice Holt Giles plumbed the emotional relationships of man and land, while Eliza Obenchain, writing in an earlier age, described the folksy aspect of the Pennyrile.

Much of the Pennyrile might well be called Kentucky's bread basket. Its broad areas of pleasantly rolling land along its southern tier of counties is reminiscent of the romantic southern plantation concept.

For more than two centuries, Kentuckians have created symbols and images to glorify their past and their heroes. The frontier with its wars and struggles created a bountiful crop of these. Standing out head and shoulders above the crowd were Daniel Boone, George Rogers Clark, Simon Kenton, James Harrod, Benjamin Logan, and William Whitley, all early pioneers. The Kentucky pantheon, however, is also crowded with heroes from other times and other wars. Nevertheless, no other Kentucky hero has attained Daniel Boone's pinnacle of fame. Fortune smiled generously on Daniel Boone. It gave him a vast, wooded country in which to roam in solitude, trails to break, Indians to fight, and a set of jealous detractors who made him famous. Fortune smiled sweetly when she sent him ghostwriter John Filson to write his autobiography, and Lord Byron to place him forever in the annals of English literature. In 1845, the Commonwealth brought his and Rebecca's remains home from Missouri and interred them on the steep knoll overlooking the state capitol. No doubt Daniel would have taken satisfaction in the continuing controversy this move generated between Kentucky and Missouri. Only the blowing of Gabriel's horn will resolve the issue of whether Daniel's remains are actually in Frankfort, on the banks of the Kentucky River, or still in Missouri.

To Kentucky came stalwart individuals who fetched along in their cultural baggage the philosophy of making do with what they had at hand. They planted a civilization which came to bear the deeply impressed stamp of the land. The Kentucky pioneers created a highly revered image of courage and sacrifice in the state and outside it, when they headed west. Into the westward movement went a blend of Kentucky-rough woodsmen, lords of pole-cabin estates, and rowdy farmer-boatmen who dealt with great hazards along the Ohio and Mississippi rivers, and struggled home over the Natchez Trace. Some of them, stimulated by the liquid contents of their cargoes, jumped up and down clicking their heels and proclaimed themselves "half horse, half alligator," "ringed-tailed roarers" charged with lightning, spoiling for a fight. Back home were the gentler mother and father figures who more truly represented the quieter way of life in rural Kentucky.

Back home too was the most persistent folk character to tread Kentucky soil: the colonel. No one can say with precise historical accuracy when this goateed creature marched onto the scene. But with several generations of active militia musters, border conflicts with Indians and British, and internal strife, it was relatively easy for a man with leadership capabilities to attain a military title by the process of social osmosis. In time, an inordinate number of Kentuckians came home from border skirmishes and wars with military titles, either earned or acquired. The ownership of a rich Bluegrass farm, a herd of purebred cattle, or a pasture full of race horses almost automatically elevated an individual to the rank of colonel. Too, Kentucky governors appointed a small army of uniformed political favorites to help perform ceremonial functions. It was almost unthinkable that a successful lawyer would go into court bearing the plain title of "lawyer"; he had at least to be a major. Today, many aspiring individuals have joined the ranks of the governors' vast army of titled gentry.

Kentucky history is full of paradoxes. One is that approximately eighty of Kentucky's one hundred twenty counties have adopted local option laws to "dry up" their jurisdictions. In Kentucky, bootleggers, moonshiners, and church people have crusaded on the same side of the local option liquor issue, with both bootleggers and moonshiners profiting from dry jurisdictions. Again paradoxically, the liquor is both amber-colored and clear as an angel's conscience. The brown-jug or fruit-jar brand was, until the repeal of the Eighteenth Amendment, the common man's drink.

From the day an unnamed Scotsman or Irishman made a run of corn liquor up the spring branch, whiskey and Kentucky have been synonymous. No historian has yet cleared the fog of mystery from bourbon whiskey's first distilling, but one thing is certain: it was not named for Bourbon County. It may have been named by the Baptist minister, Elijah Craig, of the famous Traveling Church. He first used charred-oak kegs to absorb fusil oil from raw whiskey in the Craig-Parker Mill near the Royal Spring in Georgetown. As whiskey ages in its barrels, it turns an amber color which may have suggested the royal Bourbon colors.

Still another paradox is that while Kentucky is considered the land of the horse, only a relatively small portion of the state is devoted to horse farms. Historically, the horse has always played an important role. Daniel Boone's trailblazing party in the early spring of 1775 came mounted, which accounted for their quick journey from Cumberland Gap to the Kentucky River and the future site of Boonesboro. Behind the Boone party came Richard Henderson with men, women, and children, most of them mounted on horses and leading pack animals. On their heels rode the barely literate but highly observant William Calk, who kept one of the most fascinating travel journals in western history and vividly described the treacheries of wilderness travel.

The horse was one of Kentucky's noblest pioneers. It came bearing family members, household utensils, farm tools, chickens, turkeys and geese, garden and field seeds, guns and ammunition. These yeoman animals deserve a rich bronze monument to stand alongside those of Daniel Boone, George Rogers Clark, and the other pioneers. Like Kentuckians themselves, the first horses to arrive in the Bluegrass were of mixed ancestry. There were those faithful beasts of burden who were scarcely freed of the pack saddle before they were hitched to the plow to break the land. They helped families flee Indian attacks, followed warriors in hot pursuits, and dragged logs to raise cabins and houses. They bore little relationship to those aristocrats who arrived in less servile circumstance and became sporting animals.

Early in its publication, the *Kentucky Gazette* carried advertisements of blooded and named stallions. In time, there appeared notes on racing, but not until some radical changes were made in the location of race courses. Early town charters contained clauses that forbade the racing of horses up and down main streets, making Kentucky possibly the only state in the Union where such legislation was needed. The annals of horses in Kentucky are filled with such names as

Buzzard, Diomed, Highlander, Lexington, Spread Eagle, Eclipse, and Mogul of the antebellum years. After the Civil War, the illustrious list includes Aristides, Donnerrail, Old Rosebud, Sir Barton, Man O' War, Burgoo King, Bold Venture, War Admiral, Seattle Slew, Bold Forbes, Aleysheba, and a host of others. And it would be unhistoric not to mention the heroic careers of Nancy Hanks, Patchen-Wilkes, Robin Almahurst, Arnie Almahurst, Falcon Almahurst, Greyhound, and scores of other trotters who, like the thoroughbreds, have brought sporting glory to the Bluegrass.

The lush Bluegrass pastures, palatial barns, and endless miles of whitewashed board fences symbolize for many natives, and non-Kentuckians as well, a Kentucky way of life. Since 1875, the Kentucky Derby has grown into an international sporting and social event. Annually, hostesses in Louisville and Lexington engage in lively rivalry over the most lavish pre-Derby party and the most elaborate guest list of political, entertainment, sporting, and business personalities. It was considered a coup when one couple entertained Queen Elizabeth II of England. The season at Keeneland Race Track in Lexington and that at Churchill Downs creates for many Kentuckians the most exciting

Country store along US 27, Garrard County

moments of their lives. They flock to the windows hoping they can beat the odds and go home flush.

But the horse image, like so many other images of Kentucky, is by no means universal. In sharp contrast is the comfortable image of the countryside with its small towns and villages. This is Kentucky's central image, a rural agrarian countryside dotted with farm homes, crossroad-villages, and county-seat towns, where life revolves in concentric circles about churches, country stores, courthouses, and up and down county-seat main streets. The average Kentuckian is loyal to place in the descending order of "the old home place," the county, the state, and the section. "Home" is a tremendous atavistic force which draws ex-patriots back to visit or to retire. Like Gerty Nevels of *The Dollmaker,* they carry through life visions of the "old Tipton Place" as a haven of motherly security.

Kentucky is a "mother state," whose sons and daughters often have left her to venture west. Their descendants come home to search for their ancestral roots. Literally thousands of them prowl county courthouses, the historical societies, and the state archives looking for traces of those hardy "corn patch and cabin" settlers who came west dreaming they would possess a piece of the "garden." Their names fill deed books, marriage records, wills, estate settlements, mortgages, even the civil and criminal records of the courts. Armies of plaintiffs and defendants contesting land claims went before court sessions, and the face of Kentucky is splotched by a spidery web of land claims that overlapped, or were never legally completed, as in the case of Daniel Boone.

A Kentuckian may live in towns like Paducah, Owensboro, Bowling Green, Covington, Ashland, Lexington, or Louisville, but he says he lives in McCracken, Daviess, Kenton, Jefferson, or one of a hundred other counties. The county is where he pays his taxes, buys his marriage license, and sends his children to school. He fights to maintain his county system intact. For most Kentuckians, abolishing a county would wipe out the foundation of their existence.

The Kentuckian's sense of home is intimately linked with water. Although an inland state well removed from coastal influences, Kentucky has a long history of association with springs, creeks, rivers, and lakes. Historically, the state's fortunes have depended on her water resources. The early long hunters, land speculators, and settlers sought pelts and skins, fertile land, home sites, and, always, free-flowing

Folsomdale Milling Company, Graves County

springs. Before blazing a claim or raising a cabin, a settler had first to locate a dependable source of water. This fact remains highly visible today, despite the apparently random location of homesteads.

Kentucky's rivers have ever been both blessing and curse. They formed pathways for immigrants entering the new country, relieved men and beasts of the burden of lugging goods to markets, and served as vital drainage systems for the state's craggy, steep terrain. Flatboatmen came to reflect the rugged state character. The famous Scottish ornithologist, Alexander Wilson, once climbed down the steep limestone palisade near the mouth of Hickman Creek on the Kentucky River in search of birds and saw instead a fleet of heavily ladened flatboats drifting by on their way downriver to New Orleans. He wrote, "In this deep and romantic valley, the sound of boat horns from several Kentucky arks, which were at that instant passing, produced a most charming effect . . . [and] herald a rising prosperity in the land."

But Kentucky history is also filled with accounts of floods. In 1937, Louisville was badly damaged by the rampaging Ohio, and repeatedly the Kentucky has visited Frankfort with disaster. In its gentler moments, which is most of the time, the Ohio is a lifeline. In earlier days,

thousands of immigrants have come down that stream to land at the mouth of Limestone (Maysville) Creek, the mouth of Licking, the Falls of the Ohio, and the Yellow Banks (Owensboro). Others, dazzled by the star of adventure and drawn by the availability of fresh lands, came up the Tennessee and down the Cumberland.

In 1778, a tiny group of militiamen and settlers drifted with George Rogers Clark down the Ohio to establish a safe settlement in midstream, just above the Falls of the Ohio on Corn Island. On June 24, 1778, Clark left Corn Island, floating his army over the great rock barrier into the lower river on his way to seize the northwestern forts of Kaskaskia, Cahokia, and Vincennes, and to capture the famous "hair buyer," Governor Henry Hamilton. When Clark ordered the Corn Island fort abandoned, settlers moved into the site, founding Louisville, which quickly became a major commercial port. A nameless reporter, describing its modest beginnings in 1779, related that when the first patch of wheat was raised, it was ground in a rude and laborious hand mill and sifted through a gauze neckerchief. It was then shortened with raccoon fat, and the whole station was invited to partake of a sumptuous feast of flour cake. The early Louisville historian, Benjamin Casseday, added, "How little of a prophet would he have been accounted who then had predicted that, in less than sixty years, the inhabitants of the very spot where they then stood should have at their command all the fruits and viands of every quarter of the globe."

Indeed, Louisville quickly became a rich and hospitable river city, living by and off the Ohio. In two hundred years, its residents went from sifting coarse wheaten flour through a gauze neckerchief to a modern Kentucky Derby Week, when the whole town is set aglow with several carnival events, and the surviving sternwheelers on the Ohio race to determine which can wear the buck horns for a year. Crews and passengers churn over the site of sunken Corn Island, their boats stirring the historic waters.

Here is the landing spot where their boats' awkward steam-driven ancestor, the *New Orleans,* drifted into a safe landing just above the Falls of the Ohio. Nicholas Roosevelt's smoking, belching, "infernal rig" made the downriver trip from Pittsburgh in the miraculous time of four days. On a dreary January day in 1812, Roosevelt piloted his steamboat over the flooded cataract of the Falls of the Ohio and headed downriver to open a new chapter in American transportation.

His journey south was momentous, but not quite as earthshaking as an event that occurred a month earlier. On December 16, 1811, a mighty shock roared through the lower Ohio and Mississippi river country. A witness wrote:

It seems as if the earth was afloat and set in motion by a slight implication of immense power, but when this regularity is broken by a sudden cross shove, all order is destroyed, and a boiling action is produced, during the continuance of which a degree of violence is greatest, and the scene most dreadful. . . .

Oscillating was too mild a word to describe the furies unleashed by the New Madrid Earthquake. The flow of rivers was reversed in a swirling maelstrom that hurled flatboats about like driftwood, drowning crews and sinking cargoes. So powerful were the shocks and afterwaves that the channel of the Mississippi was redirected. The upper end of Reelfoot Lake, one of Kentucky's most picturesque swampwater areas, was created and is a silent reminder that the tectonic plates might shift once again and imperil the whole valley. Interestingly, the creation of Reelfoot Lake developed a site for fauna new to the state. This is the one place in Kentucky where the noble cypress tree raises its trunk above a swollen butt and sends up breather knees above its watery roots.

The bed of Reelfoot Lake lies in the Kentucky territory purchased from the Chickasaw Indians in 1818. In October of that year, Isaac Shelby of Kentucky and Andrew Jackson of Tennessee negotiated a treaty with representatives of the Chickasaw in which the tribe ceded to Kentucky that section of the present state that lies west of the Cumberland and Tennessee rivers. Both politically and economically this was a shrewd move for Kentucky. Geographically, it balanced Appalachian highlands with a low-lying river basin corner. The addition of the Purchase not only extended Kentucky geographically and politically, it added materially to its flora and fauna. Some, like water lilies and the cottonmouth moccasin, are found nowhere else in the state. The river or delta bottoms of this southwestern tip became cotton country, and for more than a century, cotton was listed among the state's agricultural products.

Sociologically, too, the Jackson Purchase is a distinctly different region. Its people have related more closely with the lower South, and it was through the Jackson Purchase that the Confederacy first broke Kentucky's neutrality at the beginning of the Civil War, when General Leonidas Polk led his Confederate forces across the region to establish an anchorage at Columbus overlooking the Mississippi River. Here the Confederates attempted to disrupt river traffic by stretching a monstrous chain across the water. Meanwhile, across from Columbus at Belmont, Missouri, Ulysses Grant had begun his rise to success as a Union officer. Bypassing the Confederates at Columbus, he moved upstream to Paducah at the confluence of the Tennessee and Cumberland rivers. Grant's tactical decision was an important one. At Paducah, he was in an excellent position to invade the Confederacy over the two-pronged river approaches, the Cumberland to Nashville, or the Tennessee to northern Mississippi and Alabama. Capturing Fort Donelson on the Cumberland and Fort Henry on the Tennessee, he drove a federal spear deep into the heart of the South at Shiloh Church. This Union advance seriously gored the Confederacy in midcountry.

Ever since its addition to the mainland of Kentucky, the Jackson Purchase has been a crossroads. It is here that the Ohio, the Mississippi, the Tennessee, and the Cumberland converge to form a commercial and recreational network of lakes and streams, and here that the north-south railroads passed through the region, and an American folk hero was created. On the Illinois Central, the tiny village of Cayce gained national fame far beyond its importance as a fourth-class post office-country store dot on the Kentucky map, because John Luther Jones spent a part of his boyhood there. Nicknamed by his fellow railroad workers, "Casey" Jones gained immortality for himself and his village when he tried to beat the clock, and his train smashed into a freight train at Vaughn, Mississippi, on April 29, 1900. Casey saw the crash coming and told his fireman to jump; but he stayed on board, one hand on his whistle, the other on his brakes. This event seized the popular imagination and inspired one of America's most famous devil-may-care work ballads, "Casey Jones."

Another Purchase farmboy, Nathan B. Stubblefield, attained local fame as the inventor of wireless communication. As a youth, he was interested in the study of science, and especially electricity. Experimenting, he developed a storage battery, and in 1892 perfected an instrument which he used to transmit the greetings, "Hello, Rainey, Hello, Rainey." This may have been the first transmission by wireless of the human voice, and Stubblefield was granted a United States patent

for his invention. But the complicated process of obtaining a patent and trying to find a financial backer proved too frustrating for him, and he gave it up.

Nearby in Paducah, another native was to fare more successfully. Glorifying his hometown and the Confederacy in his books and stories, Irvin Shrewsbury Cobb became famous as a newspaper reporter, a novelist and short-story writer, a humorist and a moving-picture actor. In spirit, Cobb never left Paducah, always registering that address in hotels despite the fact he lived in New York. A reviewer once described him as Kentucky's chief advocate and most devoted citizen. Cobb's devotion was at least matched by his Paducah neighbor, Alben W. Barkley. Barkley was the personification of the rural Kentucky politician who climbed the ladder of fame from modest beginnings. He held local offices, then went on to the House of Representatives and the United States Senate and was elected Harry Truman's vice president. In the latter office, he became known affectionately as the VEEP.

In a different field, another Purchase native, Bobbie Ann Mason, has reached literary fame as a novelist and short-story writer. The characters of her books and stories, like Cobb's, are people of local origins

Union nurses, reenactment of 1862 Battle of Perryville

who wrestle emotionally with their past while trying to reconcile their present and anticipate the future.

The people of the Jackson Purchase, like those of the eastern highlands, generate their own folkways through the nuances of their response to their land. Time, and the particular political and economic conditions created by their location at the extreme end of a curiously elongated state, naturally set them apart politically.

Farwestern Kentucky has ever been a land dependent upon its water resources. This has been especially true since the days of the New Deal. Passage of the Tennessee Valley Authority Act, on May 18, 1933, brought about a vast reshaping of the land in western Kentucky and of a whole people's way of life. Federal legislation provided for stepping down 650 miles of the Tennessee River, from an elevation of 850 to 22 feet. Completed in 1940, the great Kentucky Dam created a long, impounded lake that reached all the way into Tennessee. The channel over which Rachael Donelson Jackson's family floated in a flatboat on their way to settle up the Cumberland at Nashville, in the winter of 1779-1780, over which Grant's army steamed on its way to Shiloh, and where hundreds of mussel-shell divers recovered rich harvests of river pearls and button materials, became a broad recreational and commercial channel. A new empire sprang up along the banks of the Kentucky and Barkley lakes. The waters of the wild Cumberland were tamed.

This was no small task. The Cumberland was an angry giant. Millions of years before, its flood waters had slashed a rock-strewn channel down from the heights of Appalachia to drain a large portion of Kentucky. Geographically, the river laces together three or four sections of Kentucky and has distinctly shaped Cumberland Valley's culture. The seed time and flowering of that culture are magnificently described in the writings of Harriette Simpson Arnow.

The Cumberland originates in Harlan County, in Appalachia, where the rugged terrain makes livelihood hard. It is impossible to deny either the richness of Appalachia's culture, which continues to be prolifically described, or the great challenge the region poses to those who would improve the statistics. "Forward in the Fifth" (Congressional District) is a rallying cry. Appalachia's strengths lie in its ties of kinship, in its people's attachment to the land, in the traditions brought to the mountains by eighteenth- and nineteenth-century pioneers, in the land itself.

Long before Kentucky and Barkley dams transformed the life and human culture in their drainage systems, that intriguing peninsula lying between them and north of the Tennessee border was the scene of a fabulous speculative venture in which plungers hoped to reap fortunes from iron and timber. Originally, this land nurtured a heavy stand of mixed hardwoods. In later days, iron masters dreamed of converting the vein of iron ore beneath the forest cover into a major American smelting industry, but this dream faded in the making. Far more profitable was the moonshine industry, which thrived during Prohibition days. Before the repeal of the Eighteenth Amendment, the village of Golden Pond became synonomous with illicit liquor running, the speakeasy, and racketeering. It was a major source of moonshine for the thirsty patrons of St. Louis and for Chicago whiskey-runners.

Golden Pond's moment of fame was brief. Repeal of the Eighteenth Amendment accomplished what the revenuers had been unable to do. Once again, Kentucky's corporate distillers offered Kentucky moonshiners too much competition. With the exhaustion of the rich timber, and the iron industry memorialized only in crumbling furnaces and abandoned mine sites, the land between the new lakes once again became home to isolated Kentucky subsistence farms.

But long stretches of transportational and recreational waters bound it tightly in a peninsula of 170,000 acres lying between Dover, Tennessee, and Kuttawa, Kentucky. It possessed virtually unlimited conservational and recreational potentials within modest driving distances of millions of midcontinent Americans. In 1963, President John F. Kennedy signed into law the bill that created the extensive natural recreational area officially designated "The Land Between the Lakes." This law prepared to return a portion of Kentucky to a near-virginal state of nature, establish a game and bird sanctuary, and open the land to controlled public access.

Before the Land Between the Lakes could be returned to a natural state, there were involved deep human emotions. It was home to almost three thousand people, and now they were forced to say farewell to it. Through generations, they had built homes, schools, country churches, stores, and post offices. On its knolls, families had buried their dead, and, perhaps most important of all, they had bonded with the land. From the beginning, life had been geared to seasons of planting and harvesting the dark leaf tobacco and the field crops, to the arrival and departure of migratory birds over the midcontinental flyway, and to the spiritual tempo of rural living. After 1963, the old way

of life began to vanish. Homesteads where several generations of peninsula Kentuckians had been born and raised were now, by law, converted into part of a recreational-forest conservation preserve.

Modern regional prophets conjured up visions of the bright new natural world-to-be and of the tourist dollars that would pour in like old-time Tennessee Valley spring freshets. They promised that the great waterways would give the people commercial connections with the world. The Cumberland would become an open boat channel to Nashville and a series of lakes beyond. The Tennessee would reach back to North Carolina, and, by way of the Tombigbee Canal, to Mobile and the Gulf of Mexico. These same arguments had been used more than a century before to promote the railroads.

Kentuckians looking backward into the two centuries of their Commonwealth's existence are now taking stock of their losses and their achievements. Confronted with a barrier of comparative statistics as dense as the stony fort of Pine Mountain, they are making new assessments of their past.

Not all of Kentucky can be converted into sparkling river impoundments, or turned into recreational playgrounds. Just as their Kentucky forebears strove to free their land of menace, their descendants are now faced with savage defacers of the countryside and with urban sprawl. The challenge to preserve home and place must be met. Writer, farmer, and conservationist Wendell Berry meets the challenge in his own Kentucky-bred way. Other Kentuckians develop other fruitful ways.

There are many achievements that reflect substantial advancement from the simpler days of rural-agrarian, social, and cultural complacency. Never before in the commonwealth's history have so many of its youth graduated from colleges and universities; never has so much help been given to adults who return and graduate from high school. For concerned citizens, the advancement of education has taken on the zeal of religious revival, and almost one hundred colleges, seminaries, and universities welcome students. Unique to Kentucky is a system of fourteen community colleges with University of Kentucky membership and close community ties.

Beyond the formal classroom door, Kentucky now has functioning a modern, effective library system. In earlier times, creaking library wagons rolled up and down country roads, taking meager offerings to book-starved readers. Today, nearly every one of Kentucky's one hundred and twenty counties has its own public library, and more than one hundred bookmobiles travel the state. From the doors of the Free Public Library in Louisville to those of Elkhorn City and Hickman, the barriers of isolation have been breached. Most heartening is the cultural and literary stimulus of the Kentucky Book Fair in Frankfort. This festival of books, which draws together authors and readers in a common bond, has become an annual exhibition of bright young authors, worthy successors to the distinguished scroll of their Kentucky literary ancestors.

The Wyandot Indians had a word for their great western reserve. They called it *Ken-Tah-Teh*, "Land of Tomorrow." This was where they hoped to live in the future. For twenty-first century Kentuckians, this is both a fitting name and a promise to carry into the future.

■ *Right:* Kentucky's diverse soils support a wealth of different plants. Here, daffodils, also known to some Kentuckians as Easter flowers, bloom profusely outside an old farm building near Dixon, in western Kentucky's Webster County. Long after farmsteads are abandoned, these hardy messengers of spring repeat their annual cycle of bloom.

■ *Left:* Redbud and dogwood bloom in eastern Kentucky's Jenny Wiley State Park. Growing with them are tall poplars, one of the state's leading timber resources. ■ *Above:* Fresh-cut tobacco stalks line a field on a foggy September morning in Oldham County. ■ *Overleaf:* Primary access to the boulder-strewn gorge of the North Fork of the Red River in Menifee County is on foot or by canoe or kayak.

■ A willow sifts sunlight through its leaves on the Headley-Whitney Museum grounds in Fayette County. Kentucky preserves its history in almost one hundred museums, including the J. B. Speed Art Museum in Louisville, the Kentucky Historical Society and Military History museums in Frankfort, the American Saddle Horse Museum in Lexington, and the Coca-Cola Memorabilia Museum in Elizabethtown.

■ The gorge of the Cumberland River below magnificent Cumberland Falls is typical of the rugged beauty of Kentucky's eastern and southern river valleys. Beginning in Appalachia, the Cumberland River slashes its bed out of unforgiving rock, then winds in a serpentine course through Kentucky heartland until it reaches the Ohio. Cumberland Falls is famous for its moonbow, which is seen at the full moon.

■ This hill farm above Clay City in Powell County sits at the western rim of the Appalachian Mountains. Near this spot in 1769, Daniel Boone and John Finley and their party of explorers first viewed the "beautiful level of Kentucky." Settlers from the eastern seaboard quickly followed, and in 1792 Kentucky broke away from Virginia and became the fifteenth state to join the Union.

■ Fly swatter in hand, Bert Summers cools off on the porch of his Jackson County farmhouse. The ninety-four-year-old farmer still tends two hundred acres of bottomland along the banks of the Middle Fork of the Rockcastle River. Porches are a Kentucky institution, gathering together family and friends in the cool of a summer evening.

■ Dawn gives rise to a foggy morning at this pay lake near Liberty in Casey County. While his two friends anticipate a strike, a third fisherman unhooks a two-pound catfish. Only Alaska has more miles of rivers and streams, and Kentuckians and their visitors make the most of recreational opportunities that last the entire year.

■ This western Kentucky farm straddles a backwater pond near the Ohio River at Bayou in Livingston County. Fertile farms contribute to Kentucky's high national ranking in agricultural production especially in the broad and rich Pennyrile region where solid agrarian culture has more than a hint of Old Cotton South.

■ A corn crib, a white fence, and a young spring willow grace the Shaker Village at Pleasant Hill, Mercer County. Founded in 1805 by disciples of Mother Ann Lee as a utopian religious society, the celibate Shakers were known as innovative crafts-people, builders, and agriculturalists, particularly during the nineteenth century. They were part of a religious revival that raised church houses all across Kentucky.

■ Rolled haystacks punctuate the early November landscape in Casey County's Green River Valley. Kentucky farms raise cattle and hogs, and produce soybeans, dairy products, and corn. Although small farms such as this have dwindled in number, they continue to play an important role in the economy of rural Kentucky.

■ *Above:* Two young men from Ohio can't resist fishing Corinth Lake along Interstate 75 in northern Kentucky's Grant County. ■ *Right:* On a soft June morning, the Middle Fork of the Kentucky River winds through Buckhorn Lake State Resort Park, near Hazard. ■ *Following Page:* Rugged terrain, in Daniel Boone National Forest near Morehead in Rowan County, stretches north and south through the heart of eastern Kentucky.

■ *Left:* Secretariat, who won the Triple Crown in 1973, earned over $1.3 million racing.

■ *Clockwise Above:* Seattle Slew won the Triple Crown in 1977 and earned over $1.2 million. Spectacular Bid won the Kentucky Derby and Preakness in 1979 and earned nearly $2.8 million. Alydar finished second in each 1978 Triple Crown race and won over $950,000. Affirmed took the Triple Crown in 1978 and earned $2.4 million.

■ *Previous Overleaf:* Steep and heavily forested ridges of the Pine Mountain Range rise from the Cumberland River Valley, near Pineville in Bell County. ■ *Left:* Miles of white fences weave across the Donerail Thoroughbred Farm outside of Lexington in western Fayette County. Horse farms have made the Bluegrass famous. ■ *Above:* A small farm pond records a sunset along Highway 527, near Lebanon in Marion County.

■ *Above:* Phlox and blue-eyed Mary border a footpath in Raven Run Nature Preserve in southeast Fayette County. Part of the Kentucky River Basin, the preserve is one of many beautiful but fragile areas which are slowly being protected through the efforts of local and state environmental groups. ■ *Right:* This tin-roofed farmhouse near Jackson, in Breathitt County, is typical of mountain dwellings in the eastern third of the state.

■ *Left:* Sunflowers line the shore of a pond in eastcentral Kentucky's Clark County. This land was once part of Indian Old Fields, *Eskippakathiki,* a Shawnee village and trading post. Indians lived in Kentucky long before settlers arrived. They created the Mississippi culture and erected vast burial mounds. ■ *Above:* Osage orange trees line a fence of oak planking along the Pisgah Pike near Versailles, in Woodford County.

■ Homemade milkshakes and sodas are still served at the Kentucky Lake Restaurant in Aurora in western Kentucky's Land Between the Lakes. Here, the proprietress quietly sips her morning coffee while waiting for the breakfast run of locals and tourists. Established in 1963 by President John F. Kennedy as a national recreation area, the Land Between the Lakes preserves 170,000 acres in a near-natural state.

■ George Slade examines one of the hundreds of varieties of irises he raises on his land in Harrison County. People come from several states to look and talk irises and to purchase some of his many prized specimens. Kentucky's geographic location provides an almost year-round climate for the growing of plants.

■ West of Frankfort, Kentucky's state capital, Benson Creek flows through central Kentucky farm country on a bright autumn morning. A tributary of the Kentucky River, the creek is one of hundreds of streams providing water to livestock and an occasional smallmouth bass to local anglers. As in days past, streams like this provide the limestone water for Kentucky's world-famous bourbon whiskey.

■ *Above:* The soft light of a foggy September morning illuminates a field of iron-weed and sunflowers. ■ *Overleaf:* Fog packs the deep valleys of Appalachian foothills on an October morning in Powell County. Hill farms and their venerable tobacco barns are scattered throughout this region of eastern Kentucky.

■ The beautiful Kentucky River and its many tributaries drain the watersheds of much of eastern and central Kentucky. This navigable stream was once a primary means of transportation, carrying meal, hogs, bourbon whiskey, tobacco, and millions of feet of virgin timber. A source of public water, it is now used mainly for boating and fishing.

■ Haystacks line a Fleming County hillside near Plummers Mill. The peaceful mid-summer scene belies a bloody history. Shawnee, Wyandot, and Delaware Indians fought here against the early pioneers. Today the county is a comfortable area of farms and covered bridges, centered around the county seat of Flemingsburg.

■ Two members of the Kentucky Chapter of the Nature Conservancy examine a plant specimen outside Bat Cave in Lee County. The non-profit Conservancy works tirelessly to find and preserve ecologically unique and endangered areas. Once a state of virgin wilderness, Kentucky is now the home of scenic, multi-lane roads and thriving towns. In this new age, nature needs some protecting.

■ Redbud, or Judas, trees color a sunny ridge in Carter Caves State Park in northeastern Kentucky. The state is riddled with limestone caves. Carved over the course of thousands of years by water, they form an underworld of lakes and rivers. Attracting casual visitors as well as serious spelunkers, they are home to many species of bat.

■ *Above:* At the golden apex of autumn, this white horse luxuriates in its sunny paddock along a country road in central Kentucky. Such idyllic scenes are common in the heart of Kentucky horse country. ■ *Right:* The rocky shore of Wood Creek Lake in Laurel County is drenched in autumn color. One of Kentucky's many man-made lakes, it produced the state's record large-mouth bass, which weighed over thirteen pounds

■ *Left:* A weeping willow stands forlornly in a Pike County meadow, the temporary victim of an exceedingly rare April snowstorm. ■ *Above:* One of Kentucky's many small churches surveys the cold of a winter's day in McCreary County. In spite of scattered congregations, a good number of rural churches survive.

■ Seat of modern Kentucky's state government, the capitol building displays elaborate marble columns and stairs. Built in 1910, the limestone structure houses the state House of Representatives and the Senate. Except for rare special sessions, the legislature convenes for only sixty days every two years. During these sessions, Kentucky oratory flows freely as public issues are debated in the capitol's vaulted chambers.

■ Autumn sawgrass edges a field in Muhlenberg County. This is part of the great western coalfield lying at the triangle of the Cumberland, Green, and Ohio rivers. Here, life on the farm goes on much as it has for the past two hundred years, and coal mining flourishes, as it does in other parts of the state.

■ Young sledders begin the return journey to the hilltop beside Grant County's Boltz Lake. Sledding days in Kentucky are rare and are taken advantage of immediately. While Kentucky lacks the severe winters of states on its northern border—Ohio, Indiana, and Illinois—it sees some snow and averages forty-five inches of rain a year.

■ Looking like a prop from a fairy tale, Letcher County's Rockvine Primitive Baptist Church sits in the midst of the state's heaviest snowfall in a hundred years. The 1987 storm left up to thirty-six inches of snow in parts of eastern Kentucky. Letcher County also boasts Lilly Cornett Woods, Kentucky's largest remaining tract of virgin timber.

■ After pitching their tent, two women sit precariously close to the edge of a sand-stone cliff in the Red River Gorge. More than a million visitors come to the gorge every year, tramping its trails, crossing its rock bridges, and exploring its rock shelters. Kentucky boasts one of the nation's largest park systems.

■ *Above:* A lone kayaker maneuvers his craft through a narrow cut in the treacherous waters of the Russell Fork of the Big Sandy River in Breaks Interstate Park. Each fall, expert kayakers gather to run this course, one of the most difficult in the eastern United States. ■ *Overleaf:* The gray trunks of Kentucky's stately poplar and the colors of young hardwoods mingle in Greenbo Lake State Park in northeastern Kentucky.

■ Because of Kentucky's relatively mild climate and its abundant farmland, Amish and Mennonites have chosen to settle in Kentucky in increasing numbers. Dressed in their traditional clothes, a Mennonite boy and his sister fetch the plow mule home from pasture in Casey County. Thrifty Amish and Mennonite families make a living from the land, using only traditional farm implements.

■ *Above:* Red sumac accents this uncultivated land in rural Lawrence County, across the Big Sandy River from the state's eastern border with West Virginia. ■ *Overleaf:* A few miles below Wolf Creek Dam, water flowing past the Creelsboro Arch along the banks of the Cumberland River in southcentral Kentucky is home to some of the state's largest trout. The river shelters jumbo rainbows and browns.

■ *Above:* Growing between solid rock, mountain laurel displays spring blooms at Natural Bridge State Resort Park in Powell County. ■ *Right:* The North Fork of the Kentucky River in Breathitt County cuts through solid rock. The rugged beauty of the upper Kentucky River basin is typical of the state's mountainous southeastern corner.

■ *Left:* Oak fences etch a snowy landscape in the heart of Bluegrass country. The neat, white barns reflect the classic sense of order that distinguishes this area. ■ *Above:* Thoroughbreds enjoy a snowy day along Versailles Pike in Fayette County. The pike connects Lexington, the "Athens of the West," with Frankfort and provides breathtaking views of some of Kentucky's famous horse farms.

■ *Above:* Almost every barn and shed in rural Kentucky has a basketball hoop nailed to it. Playing with an old Wilson leather ball, a young farmer takes a few minutes' practice in the fading light of a November day in the village of Subtle in southcentral Kentucky's Metcalf County. ■ *Right:* A farm dog waits contentedly for its master in the back of an old pickup on a small farm in southeastern Kentucky's Jackson County.

■ *Left:* Half Moon Arch glows on an October afternoon in eastern Kentucky's Red River Gorge, a magical area of rushing rivers, natural stone bridges, and an incredible range of plants and wildflowers, some on the nation's endangered list. ■ *Clockwise Above:* A lone tree grasps an outcrop above Devil's Canyon. Autumn paints a forest below Raven Rock. Sky Bridge shows its winter coat. Autumn comes to Red River's North Fork.

■ Parched Corn Overlook is just one of the hundreds of spectacular views in the Red River Gorge Geological Area. Indians walked these sandstone ridges thousands of years ago and used the many natural rock shelters for their dwellings. Rich with game, Kentucky was a hunting ground for the Shawnee, the Iroquois, and the Cherokee.

■ *Above:* Soft lighting and autumn foliage merge on Buck Creek, a tributary of Lake Cumberland, in Pulaski County. ■ *Overleaf:* Creating a fleur-de-lis at twilight, the world's largest free-floating fountain accents the city of Louisville. The fountain symbolizes the new growth taking place in Derby City, which hosts resident ballet, opera, orchestra, and theatre companies and is redeveloping its Ohio River shore.

■ *Above:* Kentucky Lake (foreground) and Lake Barkley dominate the Land Between the Lakes. Kentucky Lake is one of the world's largest man-made lakes. ■ *Right:* The Laurel River below the dam of Laurel River Lake is but a remnant of the natural gorge which held this tributary of the Cumberland River. ■ *Following Page:* High on a knoll in Johnson County lies a small mountain cemetery typical of many in eastern Kentucky.

■ *Above:* Willie Shoemaker (No. 2), one of the leading jockeys of all time, sits atop Silent King at Keeneland Race Course in Lexington on Bluegrass Stakes Day. ■ *Right:* Built in 1820, the Old Centre administration building at Centre College in Danville is the oldest continuously operating academic building in the South and joins nearly a hundred other Kentucky institutions in welcoming students from around the country.

■ *Left:* The morning sun burns through fog wreathing a woodlot on a ridge near Hickman in Fulton County. The extreme western part of Kentucky resembles the deep South and lies just three hundred feet above sea level at the New Madrid Bend of the Mississippi River. ■ *Above:* Frost-covered wildflowers complete their autumn cycle along a roadside near Hopkinsville in Christian County.

■ The *Dixie Bell* chugs along the palisades of the Kentucky River with a load of sightseers. The little vessel makes regular trips past the mouth of Dix River and under the famous High Bridge, an historic landmark. The scenic Mountain Parkway in the east, the Cumberland Parkway in the south, and the Western Kentucky Parkway, among others, have joined Kentucky rivers as major avenues of transportation.

■ Since the first pioneer farmer broke the soil of central Kentucky, tobacco farming has been a family affair. In a spring ritual, the Mitchell family in Woodford County bends over plant beds to select the best young stock. Tobacco is still Kentucky's number one cash crop, bringing in millions of dollars annually. Dark-leafed tobacco is grown in western counties. The lighter-leafed burley dominates central and eastern Kentucky.

■ A Hart County meadow in the Green River Valley lies beneath an orange coat of winter fescue. This abundant native grass is basic to haymaking and to sheep and cattle grazing. Turning brilliant green in spring, fescue is part of the cycle of land so eloquently described by Kentucky authors Robert Penn Warren and Wendell Berry.

■ In this house, now part of Lincoln Homestead State Park in LaRue County, Thomas Lincoln courted Nancy Hanks. Their son, Abraham Lincoln, was born in a one-room cabin not far away. A year earlier, Jefferson Davis was born to Samuel and Jane Davis in Todd County. One day, each man would send great armies into war: Lincoln as president of the United States, Davis as president of the Confederacy.

■ *Above:* Cypress trees flourish in a swamp in Peale Land Wildlife Management Area near the Mississippi and Ohio rivers. ■ *Right:* Yellow water primrose rims an old farm pond in the Land Between the Lakes. Fishermen know the area for its bass and croppie fishing. Hunters seek deer and wild turkey. ■ *Following Page:* Winter's silence wraps Lake Cumberland, Kentucky's most popular summer playground.

■ *Clockwise Above:* The Post Parade precedes the "Run for the Roses." Happy owners, trainers, and family members gather in the winner's circle. Churchill Downs is viewed from "Millionaires Row." Tulips bloom on Derby Day. ■ *Right:* Below the twin spires of Louisville's Churchill Downs, three-year-old thoroughbreds round the first turn of the Kentucky Derby, called the "greatest two minutes in sports."

■ *Left:* Kentuckians have a special love for their cars and trucks. This Chevrolet truck chassis rusts nobly beside a country road in Owen County. ■ *Above:* A family of cats lounges around Overbey's General Store in northcentral Kentucky's Robertson County. Plentiful in remote areas, independent stores still compete with the larger chains.

■ Millions of years of wind and rain have worn the sandstone outcropping of Auxier Ridge in the Red River Gorge into domes and bald caps. Dense forest is interspersed with sandstone projections like this to form breathtaking natural vistas. The gorge can prove dangerous to the careless, but its beauties attract an annual stream of visitors.

■ A crisp autumn morning in Johnson County in the hills of eastern Kentucky draws steam off the warm surface of Paintsville Lake. One of the many impoundments created over the past forty years, the lake brings residents and visitors days of water-sport pleasure. Johnson County lies in an area of great mineral and recreational resources.

■ Golden groundsel grows in profusion in this swampy backwater on the edge of Lake Barkley in southwestern Kentucky's Trigg County. Shallow wetlands provide vitally important habitat for a wide range of plant and animal species, including cottonmouth moccasins and mallards, black willows and cypress trees, and the American wild lotus. A little farther west lies the Purchase, a land of farms and hospitable towns.

■ The spiral staircases in the Trustees House at Pleasant Hill are outstanding examples of American folk art. Shaped like the inside of a nautilus, this stairway was designed and constructed by the young genius, Micajah Burnet. Working with native woods, he also designed all of the wood framing and construction in Shaker Village. Burnet's cantilevered meetinghouse is a marvel of architectural suspension.

■ Amish and Mennonites are creating agriculture-based communities in Kentucky's southern and western regions. Here they are able to live according to their beliefs, which include separation from the world and simplicity in dress and in worship. These Amish are traveling to Sunday services near Mattoon in Crittenden County.

■ Red clover at the height of bloom covers a hillside near Murray in southwestern Kentucky's Calloway County. While the larger cities of Louisville and Covington continue to expand industrially—and Lexington flourishes with IBM and a strong retail and service industry—scenes like this attest to the state's agrarian roots.

■ Since the early 1800s, families have buried their dead in this rugged hillside cemetery in a remote section of Clay County in southeastern Kentucky. The steep terrain is beautiful, but contributes to a somewhat difficult life. Despite, or perhaps because of, these difficulties, the region nurtures a culture rich in music and literature.

■ Confederate troops wearing authentic military dress advance on Federal positions during the annual reenactment of the Battle of Perryville, Kentucky's largest Civil War engagement. Lasting just one day—October 8, 1862—this bloody conflict involved nearly forty thousand men. Casualties came to a total of seven thousand six hundred. Some Kentuckians fought for the Confederacy; some fought for the Union.

■ *Above:* Stately homes in east Lexington exemplify the gracious life-style for which many Kentucky cities are known. It is a life-style that unites both substance and style. ■ *Right:* A courtly dogwood blooms against a sandstone cliff along White Oak Ridge in Estill County. Spring begins early in Kentucky. Snowdrops and daffodils start to bloom in March, and the season peaks in April and May.

■ *Left:* Sunrise breaks over Cumberland River Valley above Cumberland Falls, near Kentucky's southern border with Tennessee. This area of steep gorges, mountainous terrain, and rushing streams is sparsely populated. ■ *Above:* The *Belle of Louisville* and steamboats from as far away as New Orleans jam the Ohio River across from the city of Covington to celebrate the arrival of the pioneers two centuries earlier.

■ *Above:* Newly hatched fish flies hover, and a smallmouth bass takes the bait, as husband and wife enjoy fishing the Barren River near Bowling Green in the Pennyrile's Warren County. ■ *Right:* Oaks and sycamores glow in November sunlight in the Devils Canyon area of eastern Kentucky's Red River Gorge.

■ *Left:* The mountain magnolia flaunts its large, white blossoms against a stand of hemlocks in the Mead Forest Wildlife Area in northeast Kentucky's Lewis County. New magnolia blooms open in the morning and last but a day. ■ *Above:* From a ridge near Tennessee's border, farms in southeastern Kentucky's Wayne County spread northward.

■ *Above:* Winter accentuates the rugged character of this mountain hollow near Hindman in eastern Kentucky. For almost two hundred years, hollows like this have provided a frugal living. ■ *Right:* Flat land is hard to find in the eastern half of the state. This small patch of bottomland at Valley Oak in Pulaski County is highly prized.

■ *Left:* Young willows take on the yellow coat of early spring in the Tygarts Creek Valley, near Olive Hill in northeastern Kentucky's Carter County. ■ *Above:* The mimosa tree flowers on a ridge in Kingdom Come State Park in Harlan County. One of Kentucky's coal-mining counties, Harlan is a rich repository of pioneer lore.

■ One of several resident swans glides gracefully on its morning run along a dark pond in the beautiful Cave Hill Cemetery in Louisville. A river port, Louisville is commercially linked to the South and the Midwest. Founded at the Falls of the Ohio, the city is a leading manufacturer of bourbon whiskey, tobacco, and trucks and is home to the distinguished University of Louisville and *The Courier-Journal*.

■ Hedgerows and fields in Bath County near Owingsville are decked out in spring finery. The Slate Creek Valley was once famous for its iron furnaces, which prospered in the early nineteenth century. In 1814, the industry supplied cannonball to Andrew Jackson's American Army when it fought the British in the Battle of New Orleans.

■ Along the great stone spine of Pine Mountain in Appalachian Kentucky, rare Catawba rhododendron burst into color in Pine Mountain State Park. It is against this fabulously beautiful natural scene that the annual Mountain Laurel Festival is cast, culminating in the crowning of the festival queen. Nearby is Cumberland Gap, the great passageway through which thousands of immigrants entered Kentucky.

■ Bad Branch Falls in Letcher County cascades some sixty feet into a boulder-strewn gorge in a remote area near the Virginia border in southeastern Kentucky. The Kentucky Chapter of the Nature Conservancy has worked to preserve this region and its many rare plants. Increasingly, Kentucky is protecting its rich natural heritage.

■ The intense basketball rivalry between the University of Louisville Cardinals and the University of Kentucky Wildcats is reflected in a blocked shot during an annual game. For years these two national powers rarely played each other. Now they duel every year, alternating between Louisville's Freedom Hall and Lexington's Rupp Arena. The game attracts state-wide interest and a national television audience as well.

■ Personal Ensign parades before the crowd at Louisville's Churchill Downs after winning the Breeders' Cup Distaff at the prestigious 1988 Breeders' Cup races. The four-year-old filly became the first American horse to retire undefeated and uninjured since Colin in 1908. Plush Kentucky farms like Calumet, Dixiana, Hamburg, Spendthrift, and Darby Dan breed and raise Kentucky's world-famous thoroughbreds.

■ Dawn brings first light and the promise of another warm midsummer day to rolling farmland in Campbell County in northern Kentucky. A mild, temperate climate gives Kentucky long springs and falls, hot humid summers, and relatively short winters. This pastoral scene can be duplicated hundreds of times across the commonwealth.

■ The crest of Cumberland Gap, now part of Cumberland Gap National Historic Park, stands guard at the juncture of Kentucky, Virginia, and Tennessee. West of the Gap, the first long hunters found the waters of the Cumberland. Later explorers would find bituminous coal in the Cumberland ranges. Smoking with morning fog, these foothills include portions of both Kentucky and Tennessee.

■ *Above:* The bronze statue of Man O' War, at the Kentucky Horse Park near Lexington, is dedicated to one of the world's greatest racehorses. His only loss was to a horse named Upset in 1919. ■ *Right:* The C. V. Whitney mansion in Fayette County is typical of large homes in northcentral Kentucky. ■ *Following Page:* A stone bridge spans Beargrass Creek in Louisville's Cherokee Park, one of the city's many fine parks.

■ *Left:* The delicate spiderwort displays richly colored flowers near the top of 4,145-foot Black Mountain, in Harlan County. Kentucky's elevation plunges to only a few hundred feet above sea level at the Mississippi River, 360 miles to the west. ■ *Above:* Morning fog pours from Fern Lake Valley, as viewed from the crest of Cumberland Gap.

ACKNOWLEDGEMENTS

My thanks go to Douglas A. Pfeiffer and Graphic Arts Center Publishing Company for their faith in me; to IBM Lexington and its employees for permission to use the photograph chosen for the cover, which they commissioned from me in 1983 to commemorate their achievement in quality; to Dr. Thomas D. Clark, who wrote the wonderful text for this book; to David Martin, Tim Briggs, Connie Cornelison, Lee Oliphant, Linda Gosnell, Marilynn Archambeault, and Regena Balazs.

To my father and mother, John and June; to my step-mother, Esteleen; and to my sister, Kathy, and my brother-in-law, Bennett — my gratitude.

JAMES ARCHAMBEAULT